MW00939839

Noesis

Empowering the God in You: Book #1

Author: Jay Noetic

Noesis

Defined

Noesis-

1. (Philosophy) the exercise of reason, especially in the apprehension of universal forms.

2. (Psychology) the mental process used in thinking and perceiving; the functioning of the intellect. See also cognition

Cognition

1. The mental process of knowing, including aspects such as awareness, perception, reasoning, and judgement

2. That which comes to be known, as through perception, reasoning, or intuition; knowledge.

Noesis

Table of Contents:

- ***Cognition 1***: "Your revolution might not be televised, but it can be broadcasted with one solitary sound wave, your voice."
- ***Cognition 2***: "Life is a canvas, we are the artist. It will only be as beautiful as the artist who lays the strokes to the canvas."
- ***Cognition 3***: "Let your actions speak deeper meaning than your words and let your words initiate stronger movements than your actions. "
- ***Cognition 4***: "Your desires and dreams are one in the same with The I am. Live your life, express your ideas and live your dreams. Don't waste another day wishing you had."
- ***Cognition 5***: "People shouldn't be allowed to come and go as they please in reference to your life. It should be your decision or a

mutual agreement, not their agreement forced upon you. Convenient means "suited for personal comfort." If it's convenient for them and inconvenient for you, make a decision to conveniently show them that they are either here or there but not both."

- *Cognition 6*: "Sometimes your best shot won't make the goal."

- *Cognition 7*: "The Truth about the law of attraction? It's not just speaking it into existence, it's also doing it into existence. Be your attraction."

- *Cognition 8*: "Your struggle was brought on by your decisions, and so is your success."

- *Cognition 9*: "Tough conversations need to be had with other people but none more important than the tough conversations that you need to have with yourself."

- *Cognition 10*: "Stop confusing being fearful with waiting on God."

- *Cognition 11*: "Anger is so powerful that it convinces you that it's okay to spew hate towards the very people in the same struggle as you."

- *Cognition 12*: "Half of your problems are a direct result of ignoring problem number one."

- *Cognition 13*: "At some point in your life, you have to get tired of the stagnation. You have to finally decide to stop making decisions for yourself that are based upon how someone else will feel."

- *Cognition 14*: "Weaknesses are strengths that you haven't learned to master."

- *Cognition 15*: "Make your present as nostalgic as you remember your past to be."

- *Cognition 16:* "One day you'll have to go to war with false self to allow authentic self to live without turmoil."

- *Cognition 17:* "God never left you or casted you out of which you came, but you've been taught that you were born into less than when in fact you're more than what you can possibly imagine."

- **_Cognition 18:_** "You can live your entire life believing in beliefs. Defining yourself by concepts that are true and untrue, but there is only one belief lived by you that you can truly call real and that's the belief in yourself."

- **_Cognition 19:_** "The future now is fluid, and like liquid, it spills in many different directions when spilled on the table."

- **_Cognition 20:_** "Facts will never matter to the people who believe their beliefs are indeed facts."

- **_Cognition 21:_** "If only I could remain as free as a child I'd be able to question everything and conquer the world in the same breath."

- **_Cognition 22:_** "Pain, disappointment, and sorrow are the ingredients for understanding self."

- **_Cognition 23:_** "If your words can't speak as clear as your actions then your actions won't be heard."

- **_Cognition 24:_** "The toughest pill you'll have to swallow is the belief in the worthiness of yourself. No matter how hard it gets in the different aspects of your life you must be your biggest champion, cheerer, and supporter."

- ***Cognition 25:*** "Inner peace can never be interrupted by others, but that won't stop them from trying to give you a glimpse of hell."

- ***Cognition 26:*** "Inner peace can never be interrupted by others, but that won't stop them from trying to give you a glimpse of hell."

- ***Cognition 27:*** "Built a temple that I owned and learned that I had to fix everything that was broken within it."

- ***Cognition 28***: "We were Good enough believing we weren't Good enough; so we struggled to stop the self-sabotaging stuff."

Foreword

By: Certified Life and Leadership Coach of
InspHigher, Bridgette Simmonds

Imagine a man who picks up and moves to an entirely new city over 700 miles from home – without knowing anyone – in order to grow and become even more aware of who he is as a man. That's a man who knows who he is and is unafraid to continue searching for more of his inherent power and alignment.

That man is Jay Noetic and many years ago, I met him shortly after he relocated to the Tampa Bay area. The most interesting part about Jay is that you would not know that he just picked up and moved here without knowing anyone by the way he was able to authentically and lovingly connect with me and others who called the place home many years before he arrived.

His way of being, his thoughts and profound wisdom about life was infectious and it did not take him much time to create a sense of community that many of simply enjoyed what he would create.

Noesis

Thankfully Jay's creations have not been limited to only a select chosen few in our beloved city as Jay has so powerfully shared his thoughts about life and a life well-lived in his latest book, *Noesis*.

Every one of us is a complex and varied potpourri of the thoughts, beliefs and expectations of our environment. From the time we were born, we received messages and were even rewarded – and punished – for doing things the "right" way and the "wrong" way according to what "right" and "wrong" mean in our family of origin and eventually our family and friends of our choosing (which ironically often match our family of origin!) As a result, we tend to reach this place where some of us wonder, "is this who I really am?" or "is this who I was created to be?"

In Jay's magnificent book *Noesis*, through each chapter – or Cognitions as he calls them – sheds light on a way of being that aligns you to your true nature. Jay poetically and powerfully and with so much love allows you to ask yourself the best questions that unwrap you from any covering that inhibits you from living in a state of true and total freedom.

It's in these Cognitions you get to have a meeting with your Creator to understand your greatest and best use and purpose and discover if how you think and how you feel and how you BE is actually truly YOU. It's a book on becoming. Becoming clear. Becoming love. Becoming powerful. Becoming more of who you are. That is, after all, one of the two greatest questions we all seek to answer in life – who am I and why am I here? If you have ever wondered any one or both of these things, *Noesis* MUST be at the top of your reading list!

This may sound like a tall order to be met in a simple book, however in my years of being a Certified Life and Leadership Coach, it is certain that the better questions you ask of yourself, the more clarity you find in the finding of yourself. To put it simply, this book is everything you need to discover everything you TRULY are!

Noesis

Introduction

The *ensō* symbolizes absolute <u>enlightenment</u>, strength, elegance, the universe, and <u>*mu*</u> (the void). Creation of an ensō symbolizes a moment in time in the life of the artist when the mind is free to simply let the spirit create through the physical body.

The words you're about to read in the following cognitions were created by the God me, which is not to be confused with whatever the creator of all is. There is a difference but not enough to discredit your power.

 So don't be offended by the use of language calling you and I God. We are not The God but God is in all of us, and it's the God in me that's connected with The Creator that allowed my free mind to understand that which was within me and essentially you as well.

Noesis

It's been three years since the publishing of The Unbelievable Truth: A Guide To Finding Peace and during those three years, I've experienced the most clarity that I've ever had in my time on earth. You may be asking yourself, "*Why did it take Jay so long to write this book*? "And the honest answer is life happened.

Truth be told I couldn't write new material for the book when my personal life was not aligned with what I needed to be happiest in the right now moments. I needed a different job, I needed a loving relationship, I needed to be debt free or at the very least not stressed about finances, and I needed a better understanding of life.

No matter the moment in time; I did know that I wouldn't and couldn't give you information birthed from within me while I was frustrated with life situations that I had put myself in. I truly believe all words written or spoken that teaches spiritual growth should be given when the teacher is in a place of love, clarity and personal truth and not while angry, sad and undecided.

Noesis

I didn't allow this to stop me from blogging on anoeticlife.com and I didn't allow life to stop me from my spiritual growth; in fact, I'm not sure anything in life can stop my spiritual hunger for growth which is why I grow exponentially each year because of my spiritual practices.

During my three-year journey, I listened deeply to the God in me and learned to empower "my God" so that I could be a vessel that helps other people find their own voice, own life, own peace and their own God within. I took notes, I questioned everything and broke my life apart to reassemble it the way it worked best for me. It was in this re-alignment that I discovered the following understanding of the cognitions in this book.

There are 28 cognitions in book 1, and you can call these cognitions life lessons if it suits you better, but whatever you call them do not call them false. There's nothing false about the words that are about to empower the God within you and I hope that with each cognition read you'll feel more grounded in who you are or who you want to be. I'm the teacher in this book, and I write these words first so that I alone can shoulder the full force of the cursing and ridiculing that comes with "thinking different."

You've earned every word that's in this book, and you're owed the change that you're about to bring into your life. I know you're tired of following the rules that no longer fit in your life because like you; the world is changing.

Change is always scary because when we evolve, we don't always know what's on the other side of the walls we just tore down that was "protecting" us all the years prior. The fortunate news for you is that if it gets too scary, you can always go back to what you know.

But I have a feeling that once you embrace the words in this book and take ownership of your life that you won't want to go backwards because you'll understand that there's nothing back there for you.

What you'll find going forward in the next pages and at the beginning of each cognition are quotes that I created. The words beneath that quote are the words that explain how to apply that quote to your life.

Noesis

Like in life, things rarely happen in the order we think it should, and the great thing about this book is that you don't have to read the cognitions in order. You can read this book from back to front, front to back, middle to front and then go back or whatever order you feel best fits your mood.

This book was written to be an easy read, a quick read and a discussion book. Grab a partner, grab a friend and read a cognition daily or weekly. Have an authentic conversation about each cognition and even debate if you must. What does your soul say when you read the cognitions? Well; without further ado; it's time to empower the God in you and now let us begin.

Noesis

Cognition 1:

"Your revolution might not be televised, but it can be broadcasted with one solitary sound wave, your voice."

There will come a moment in your life when you'll stop to look back at the life you've lived. During this reflection, you'll likely see that much of your time is spent trying to fortify your life around the justification of others. What I mean by this is that if you look closely at your life, you'll notice that you speak like other individuals, dance like other people and even at times carry your daily life like others.

I'll go on record and say that this isn't always a bad thing to do in your life but (and there seems to always be a but) you as a spiritual being are encouraged to do a better job at making sure you're implementing and truly understanding individuals who will help better your life and not hamper them or damage them.

To be frank; to reach higher levels of pure consciousness, you must make sure that you find a balance between someone else's voice and your own. After all, what a sad life it would be if the voice that comes out of your mouth is unrecognizable.

If you can't recognize the voice that comes out of your mouth, then it opens the door to lose your way, lose your life vision and lose your self-identification. You can look around at our society and see that the majority of people no longer have their own voice. They broadcast loudly the beliefs that have been thrust upon them by parents, friends, media or the church.

The individuals that choose to broadcast in their own belief system, their own voice are often looked upon as either Geniuses, specially gifted or slightly off their rocker. Most of our society has lost respect for authentic revolutionaries and now praise those individuals speaking the same things as themselves. But where is the growth in that?

Noesis

In the search for finding peace, many individuals have decided that it's better to fit in instead of standing out. It's possible that you yourself have turned into this individual you no longer understand.

You've likely turned yourself into an even more complicated ball of mess by trying to adopt everyone else's thought process, but they're in direct conflict of your own personal beliefs, so it leaves you spiritually torn.

This happens to all of us because we learn from those who raise us and as I mentioned we also learn from those in our circle of friends. When you're growing from an infant into an adolescent, you learn to speak with their voice.

You don't have any control over this process; this is the way of life, to learn from who may be able to teach us, to teach you. Your friends and family influence you and you influence them. The topics and beliefs that sound correct to you in that moment of life, you adopt into your life. All that you can do is to embrace this and then modify it.

Noesis

Influencers are not necessarily wrong in what they teach you, but it's best to say that you should never take things at face value. Always ask yourself the tougher questions, always dig deeper than the surface level criteria. Ask yourself, is what they're teaching you based on facts or belief? Is what you teach someone else based on facts or simply what was passed to you?

It's up to you to decide what you allow into your spirit, it's up to you to decide what is fact and what is fiction. What are you broadcasting in your circles? What are you teaching your network of friends and family?

Unbelievably; it's important for you to find what resonates deeply within you as truth and to never be afraid to challenge that truth as you continue to exist in life; because who you decide to be is what you will be remembered as. You are remarkably beautiful, and your voice can change lives for the better or for worse, this is only one of your powers in this world.

Fill your spirit with knowledge that can move mountains. Trust that the time for surface level information has passed. The world is always changing, and it's time for you to change with it. You are a uniquely created being who was never meant to march to the drumbeat of others.

It will benefit you to remember that your voice is powerful, unique and refined. It's time that you stop speaking a language that you truly don't understand. What this means exactly is that you as an authentic individual will have to think for yourself, fact find for yourself and quite possibly go against the grain by yourself.

However, know that the road less traveled doesn't always have to be a lonely one as we are often quoted as saying. The road less traveled can be filled with individuals walking the same path of truth-seeking that you're marching to.

To find these people, it does require stepping outside of your comfort zone, it requires you to color outside the lines, and it requires you to think freely. To broadcast in your own authentic voice, the walls that you've built must be torn down. This is one of the ways that you find true peace, by deciding that you'll live this life your way.

The question is, does this mean that you can't take any advice from others? Absolutely not! It's not possible for one individual to know all things. We as human beings will never know it all or be able to gather all the information we need by ourselves to grow to the levels that seem out of reach.

If the goal is to reach new heights, you must surround yourself with individuals who "get it" or study materials on the subject that you desire to grow in. Don't fall for the belief that "there is nothing new under the sun." Yes, most information is simply rediscovered, but it takes brave individuals to discover what has yet been found.

Rediscover your voice today by not allowing the worries about what others think of you or about you to be no more. Be a rebel to possibly discovering new ideas, new thoughts and possibly a new belief system that is more in tune to how you feel inside. Many people will not be able to hear the new frequency that you'll be operating in.

This list includes lovers, family, and friends but it's important to recognize that this too is okay if they don't get it, it's not your responsibility to make them "get it," it's only your responsibility to love them for where they are in their life without placing expectations onto them.

Revolutionary people don't expect people to change just because they say so; they simply believe that by living as an example of authentic living that the rest of the world will reconnect with that energy radiating out of them.

Our world is changing, and many people are looking to be nurtured with true knowledge and authentic leaders. These individuals who lead have a responsibility to stand out from the crowd by speaking in their own true voice. Are you one of these leaders? You can be if you so desire, but you must start dialing into the frequency you so wish to broadcast to the world right now.

Your desire to find balance in life will begin when you start speaking in the only voice that matters; yours. The questions that many people ask me is,

Noesis

"how do I know if it's my own voice that is speaking?" How do I know if it's my own path that I'm walking?" Honestly? When you put forth the effort, time and practice in understanding yourself, you won't have to second guess your voice and path because truth will always feel like peace.

<u>Cognition 2</u>

"Life is a canvas, we are the artist. It will only be as beautiful as the artist who lays the strokes to the canvas."

The spiritual life that you live here on earth is an amazing experience, and it should always be in your best interest to learn how to see the beauty that exists all around you in your present moments. The future now will take care of itself when it arrives, but the present moments can be as fleeting as a Florida Autumn if we don't learn to enjoy them.

Very often when it comes to how people live they fai to see the beautifulness that exists in their life. In fact, they most often wait to see the beauty that exists near the last years of living. And yes, while it is better late than never for this to occur, the truth is that it doesn' have to be this way.

Noesis

It's easy to forget that you and I are co-creators of this place we exist in. While it is true that we ourselves did not first design earth, it is equally true that we're now molding earth quicker each year. For better or for worse (whichever perspective you decide to take) we have had a part in what we see all around us.

The even more amazing fact of the matter is that we're creators of our own lives; a fact that is always overlooked. We can do or not do whatever it is we desire, although some of the greater things in life that we yearn to achieve are harder to accomplish, it too can be done.

Understand this power statement; you are the painter who applies the strokes to the canvas. You can no longer forget that fact. And more importantly, you must stop allowing other people to paint for you. The most talented artist in the world typically does not hire someone else to paint their self-portrait. No, they know what they want and how they want to look. They paint their picture by themselves; which if I must be honest, blows my mind.

Noesis

Reader, I want you to blow my mind by showing me that you understand that it's your time to express the energy that exists inside of you. It's time the entire world learned the absolute truth about the power from within.

While many believe we aren't The God, we are part of God and therefore are Gods on earth. This sounds like blasphemy I know. The mere thought of calling yourself a God makes you feel like you're committing a sin, but it's not a sin to know yourself as greatness.

You cannot be part of something and not be it. It is impossible to be mixed with different parts but only accept one part of it. To deny part of what you are is to tell yourself a lie. A child that is half black and half white cannot honestly say "I am black" or "I am white"; no, that child must say he/she is mixed with or a combination of.

We all are mixed with something and cannot truly state that we're one hundred percent of anything. Even your human body is made up to fifty to seventy percent of water, and the rest are other elements. Could you deny the other thirty percent of yourself?

Can you deny the parts of God that exist inside of you?

My point is this; God (whatever God is) was and is an artist, look at the earth God created, look at the universe God created and look at yourself which God created. God creates beautiful things! This creator gene exists in you as well.

The parts of God that exist in you are what makes you unique, and these are the parts of you that need to be released. The most famous book in the world says, "created in the likeness of God"; yes you are!

As I stated, this truth about being Gods here on earth is often looked upon as blasphemy because many people believe that God will punish them for thinking this way, but this isn't true. The universe loves you and accepts you for who you already are and who you're becoming. There is no punishment for being what you are; there is no sin for doing what you're designed to do.

Your life will be much more fulfilled when you learn how to separate the beliefs that have been taught to you from the facts that exist. Don't get rid of your beliefs but understand when a mixture is needed, and you'll see this to be true about true fulfillment. If you want to find a deeper peace and a better connection with God, you don't have to lose your beliefs you just need to understand them in its full context.

You are Gods, and the only reason you don't live and enjoy it as such is because your egos combined with your beliefs make it hard to fathom and see, therefore making life unable to be enjoyed fully.

Do you want to enjoy more of your life? I'm sure you do and sometimes you need to start over and sometimes it's simply time to move on to another chapter, another canvas. You've been given not just one blank canvas but multiple blank canvases.

This is the only truth that we know about life. This is not a belief, this is a fact. God has given you free will free control, FREE-dom. You can decide to paint your life how you so choose to see it. Does that not make you God of your life? God on earth?

Noesis

Understand, no one knows how The I AM manifested the idea of planet earth. No one knows how The Everything figured out the perfect balance to sustain life. All that we do know is that The Alpha and Omega had a vision and in that vision, she created all that we know and see. With each stroke that God made, the picture on the canvas began to form. Through that beautiful vision of seeing life exists on earth, you were allowed to be conceived and created in time.

Likewise, no one knows how you envision your life, your world. No one knows how you will find the perfect balance to sustain your life, but your canvas is your life that you choose to live and with every stroke that you make you begin to form a picture on that canvas. You too can be a visionary artist like Salvador Dali. You to have an opportunity to show the world your vision.

Will your life canvas be abstract, Primitivism, Realism or Surrealism? They all are beautiful, and all are as beautiful as the artist who paints it. Show the world your vision. Here is the beauty of this life that we live; if you don't like what you see or what you have created, you can start over with a new plan. If you truly desire to live the rest of your life in the peaceful manner that you seek, then I encourage you to stop coming up with reasons why you can't and start coming up with reasons why you can.

There are plenty of reasons why you should, but there is only one crucial reason that matters before the rest. And it's the reason you are reading this book. You desire more. If you desire more, reader, then go get more. More happiness, more money, more love, more life-changing events. They won't just fall into your lap. See the vision and put the vision into action and watch it form into the beautiful life that you yearn for.

Cognition 3

"Let your actions speak deeper meaning than your words and let your words initiate stronger movements than your actions. "

What separates great leaders from everyone else? What traits do they have that other people don't? Why do many people like Tony Robins, Barack Obama and Oprah Winfrey seem destined to lead? Are they destined to be inspirational? Are they charismatic people? Is it because they know something that you don't about leadership?

The answer to these questions is that it's a combination of all these things, but you can have a mixture of all these things as well. Truthfully, the main reason some people become great leaders and others do not, is because those who become these great leaders believe deeply about their ideas, products, and beliefs and are willing to die trying to become successful doing what they're passionate about.

These magnificent leaders believe they can change the world with what they know, do or create. If you pay close attention, you'll see that the passion that great leaders possess burst through the seams in the words they speak when in front of people. More importantly, they don't simply lead by their words, they lead by their actions. These great leaders go out and do, not just say. They truly lead by example with their actions and then allow their words to follow suit.

As I mentioned, all of you reading these words have the capability to do this, but you just haven't tapped into the right source yet. You reader have the capability to become great leaders if you so desire. Leadership at times scares many people but don't let i scare you.

Don't be afraid of the task at hand before you even get started or before you even know what it takes.

Noesis

Yes, with leadership comes greater burdens, this is a certainty no matter the size of the following. However, being a great leader doesn't necessarily equate to having to lead millions. It may simply mean being a great leader to family, friends, associates, co-workers and your significant other.

This is the mark of a great leader, leading others to a higher awareness, to a higher consciousness and encouraging others to change lives. And guess what? There isn't a shadow of doubt in my mind that you aren't able to lead your peers. Why? Because we're all bred from greatness.

To become a great leader, you must first have a desire to help others. Most people already have this desire in them, and if I had to go out on a limb, I'd say that you possess this as well. You were created to help others along your life journey, so this comes second nature for you.

Another ingredient for becoming a great leader is that you must also find something that you're passionate about. Let me ask you, what are you passionate about? No seriously, think about that question. What are you passionate about? Think about the things that you're extraordinarily good with, and I mean really good with and then ask yourself, "how can this passion benefit someone else?"

There's a leader inside of you, and there's someone who needs to be led. But here's the catch, people won't follow you just because you speak well. People follow those who are genuine in their approach, life, and actions.

If you want to become the great leader that's inside of you, ESPECIALLY in the field that you're passionate about then it will require you to be authentic. Authenticity breeds positivity and positivity evokes change. Let's work on changing you before asking people to follow you.

One of the best practices for working on your leadership qualities is to work on influencing the people in your life who you have direct contact with. Do the people in your life listen to what you say? Do they emulate what you do? Do they ask you for advice? If not; there is likely a reason behind this.

Sure, maybe they're stubborn but also; maybe they don't trust you to lead them.

Maybe your actions don't align with what you say. Remember what I said about great leaders. They passionately do, and they passionately say. Are you passionately doing or are you just passionately saying? It can't be one or the other for authentic leadership.

Here's a little golden nugget for you to remember. It's easy for people who don't know you to believe in you, but it's harder for those who know you to do so. If you can heal broken relationships in your personal life, then you'll be able to convince others to follow you as well.

You're destined for greatness, and someone is waiting for you to show them what great leadership looks like so don't keep them waiting. Whatever it is that you're passionate about, let it shine through so brightly that the sun itself wonders if it gave birth to you.

Don't let any spiritual beings that you call friend, family, and foe to deter you from your leadership capabilities; there is a leader in you. All of you can be great leaders if you practice, listen, do and listen some more. Shadow individuals who you admire and apply their characteristics to your leadership qualities and you'll become what exists inside of you already. Ex-General Electric CEO Jack Welch once said, "*Before you are a leader, success is all about growing yourself. When you become a leader, success is all about growing others.*

This is the ultimate truth in regard to being a leader. Grow yourself before you try to lead others because only fools follow the person who's the same today as they were yesterday. I can testify that there isn't anything more powerful to followers than a leader who can not only talk about what needs to be done but can relate to what was done before and how they can completely understand where the follower is currently in life.

Noesis

Cognition 4

"Your desires and dreams are one in the same with The I Am. Live your life, express your ideas and live your dreams. Don't waste another day wishing you had."

Have you ever awoken from a dream and said, "I wish that really happened?" Yes, no? It's perfectly okay to admit the truth if you have. Truth is; everyone at some point in their life used these words in one form or another.

Whether a person said it after they awoke from a sexual dream in which they were enjoying the pleasures of it or awaking from a dream where they were having a conversation with an ex-love in which they realized they missed; you have likely uttered those words.

Here is an unfortunate fact that I'd like for you to avoid, every year thousands of people close their ey never to awake again and in those last moments mo of those people say, "I wish I had done more." The take with them great ideas and big dreams that neve made it out of their minds, never out of fantasy into reality. This doesn't have to be you if you would quite simply treat your ideas and dreams as God asking you for a favor of expression through you.

Who wouldn't want to do God a favor if it were possible? Why wouldn't you want to do God a favo Everything that you do here on earth is an opportunity for you to allow your spirit to allow Go to experience itself through your actions and especially through your desires.

It's true that not every dream will be able to be mad into reality obviously, but I only use the analogy of dreaming to hammer home a point that your real-li dreams don't have to be a figment of your imagination.

Remember that some of the most world-changing creations started off as crazy ideas from someone's imagination. The difference between those who took that crazy idea and made it a reality versus the people who did not is minuscule; we're talking microscopic. In fact, if you trust in your intellectual self that tells you that anything is possible you'd have most of the things in your life that you desire and dream of. You're a dreamer with big goals and big ideas, but because life has been challenging for you, you haven't taken enough risks on making your dreams come true. And if you've taken a risk on them, there hasn't been enough follow through.

Remind yourself that you need to take more risks in achieving your desires and dreams. While all of you may not have been born with the same opportunities, all of you were born with the same magnificent DNA Genomes (with a slight variation). Which means, reader, that you aren't any different than the people creating mobile apps and startup companies.

No different than the people writing bestselling books, directing movies and/or creating awe dropping inventions. It may take you a little longer to make your dream a reality but trust and believe that you can achieve it.

Noesis

Typically, the question that comes next is "How will I know if the dreams and desires come from God? And I typically answer with, "How do you know that they don't?" Spiritually speaking, you can never truly know that it's God that gives you some of your desires and dreams. You most likely have been manipulated in some shape or another by the world around you, and sometimes that manipulation leads individuals to believe that they desire something that they truly do not.

To be more certain than not about following your dreams and desires, I encourage you to dissect and study each desire and dream as if your life depended on it. Always trust in your Noetic self before making a decision based on what you feel. Once you begin understanding the why's and why not's of each of your dreams and desires then you can begin to eliminate the dreams and desires that don't feel like they came from the higher power.

Intellectually understand, then emotionally comprehend and whatever dreams and desires that remain afterwards, then you should go with both fee forward with no looking back. Trust in this; looking back at where you came from while still on the current journey will only benefit those who are trying to keep you where they are.

Anyone or anything that desires to be beneficial for you will need to do their part to catch up. There should never be a "hold on wait for me" situation in reference to your dreams. Never believe that there will ever be anything beneficial for you in the past that will take you where you are trying to go. Go forward with no remorse, go forward with no qualms, just…..go…..forward.

It will make me happier knowing that you're living and experiencing your desires and it would make you happiest by doing so. The universe has created everything that you need in yourself in order for you to experience all that there is and all that there is; is everything.

The only thing that you have to do to experience everything is to learn the actions to achieve it and then once you do, apply it. That will be the challenge, reader; that will be the ultimate test; will you be able to apply it? Dreams and desires don't go from fantasy into reality without constant application.

I can't make many promises to you, reader, about the current lifetime that you're living in but I can promise you this; you will never regret doing something that you love, and that is an absolute truth that transcends time. Do what you love unapologetically, eloquently and faithfully. In reference to careers, I suggest that you only go back to doing something that you don't love when you've exhausted all opportunities to be successful at doing what you do love. Some people will teach you to never go back, but you also have a responsibility to yourself to not struggle financially. If at some point you're no longer able to sustain what you need then you must regroup, rethink and rebuild. And that sometimes means going back to a job that you don't care much for in order to maintain livability.

Stay encouraged.

Noesis

Cognition 5

"People shouldn't be allowed to come and go as they
please in reference to your life. It should be your
decision or a mutual agreement, not their agreement
forced upon you. Convenient means "suited for
personal comfort." If it's convenient for them and
inconvenient for you, make a decision to
conveniently show them that they are either here or
there but not both."

I want nothing more for you than for you to be
happiest in every moment that you experience here
on earth. You deserve the best in every aspect of your
life, and I believe that soon you'll begin to hold your
self-worth in as high regard as you do with your
appearance. You're a beautiful being inside and out
but sometimes (maybe too many times) you are
emotionally messy, maybe even emotionally ugly. My

desire for you is not to stop you from being emotional but to help you balance the emotional part of your being in an effort for you to make better decisions about your life.

You're an emotional, spiritual being who often makes decisions about their life based on how you feel. This isn't a bad thing at all but making decisions based on feelings you don't understand will often lead you off the path you desire for yourself.

All spiritual beings do this and honestly speaking, what a person feels can often lead them to make a decision that takes them years to recover from if their decision is based solely on what they feel in those present moments. Can I ask you a question? Do you think it's possible to be happiest in every aspect of your life? Sure you can!

Truthfully it's likely impossible for most, due to the fact that it requires a level of spiritual consciousness that many will struggle to achieve. If you can achieve this Christ consciousness, then please do so but if you come up shorter than planned just remember that you must experience unhappiness in order to truly appreciate what happiness is. Find peace in this because sometimes coming up short in certain situations is the only option; I understand this, and I'm sure you understand this as well, even if you aren't aware of it at this moment.

When these moments happen, and you're in your feelings, make no sudden decisions. Be present, be aware be still before making decisions. There are many experiences that could be avoided in your life if you stood firm in what you don't allow to exist in your life. Specifically speaking in this cognition, I'm speaking of other human beings who only come and go in your life when it suits them. Where does the blame for this lay? With them or with you?

I know it's easiest to put the full blame on the individuals who come and go as they please but what's the truth? The truth is, you're the one who continues to allow these individuals in your life. It's very true that people can only do what you allow them to do to you, so in a sense, you're torturing yourself by allowing the actions.

Self-torture is ten times worse than someone else trying to destroy your life because most often when you're torturing yourself, it's hard to see a way out because the self-doubt clouds your vision far worse than what anyone else can do to you. It's easier to see what others do to you than it is to see what you do to yourself but the common denominator in all of your human relationships is you. You have to do better before the people who come into your life are better.

 The people who come and go like the east wind aren't capable of staying committed to anyone; their issues run deep. This uncertainty of what they want causes destruction in every life they touch. Unfortunately, many people give these same people the keys to the bulldozer, and I'd like to see you and anyone else do better in this department of your life.

Now, many of you likely had thoughts about intimat relationships when thinking about this knowledge an topic, but I'm not speaking specifically about the mer and women that you date, marry and have sexual intercourse with.

These opportunists will also disguise themselves as your family and friends, and unfortunately, they thrive on your emotional messiness, and they won't stop until they have either drained your spiritual energy or that the door has been closed completely. As you can probably comprehend, your best option is to be the one who closes these openings before they drain your energy because if you don't, they'll wait until you have refilled your energy and come back in that fulfilled moment to drain it again. They are what's called spiritual leeches, and you'll never get to the place you desire with them existing in your life in their current form.

I strongly encourage you to begin having conversations with the people who bring you down and bring you out of your natural, peaceful element. I can't emphasize enough that you begin removing individuals who have proven to you that they have no desire to be part of your life long-term.

Before you shut the door on them for good, make sure that you have authentic conversations with them about why the current state of your relationship is no longer working and why you must move on from the relationship in its current form.

Once these conversations are completed, and there still isn't any change in the person or people's actions towards you, then it's in your best option to remove them from the equation of your happiness. Remember, that this life is about finding and experiencing love, peace, and happiness.

You're a highly intelligent spiritual being, and you absolutely know what's good for you and what's not. Your emotions can't always get the best of you and more often than not, your emotional messiness is what keeps bringing the opportunists back into your life.

This emotional messiness often blinds you from seein which individuals aren't beneficial for you and until you're emotionally uncluttered, this holding pattern of discontent will continue. Take ownership of your emotional ugliness and watch your relationships grow exponentially because of it. The question is, how do one properly do this? The first thing to do is learn to understand what you're feeling.

Noesis

Truth is, what you feel is often second to what you've been thinking. And what you've been thinking doesn't necessarily mean that's what you feel. Your ego if not understood will lead you to believe that they are truly one and the same. Overthinking can lead to chemical reactions in your brain that then tell the rest of the body how to feel.

 For example; anxiety surrounding certain topics can cause chemical imbalances in your brain. So when you're feeling lonely, it's likely because you've been thinking about something that then led you to feel what you feel and then you do something that brings the spiritual leeches into your life because you're in an unhealthy emotional place all because of your thoughts.

Don't be controlled by your thoughts any longer, don't be controlled by your ego anymore. It's time for you to stop allowing people who don't uplift you to continue to exist in your life. Aren't you tired of it? Aren't you tired of the negative energy these people bring? Well, it starts with you! It starts with you learning to control your emotions. It starts with you being able to identify when you're becoming emotionally messy and stopping it in its tracks.

People can't exist in your life when it's convenient for them and inconvenient for you, and they certainly shouldn't exist when it's inconvenient for both you and them, but they will certainly try to exist if they can see even the slightest amount of renewed energy coming from you. Become stronger emotionally so that when these leeches come seeking that which is not theirs, you'll be able to protect yourself before they are even able to latch on to you.

Stop over thinking and stop thinking yourself into loneliness, sadness, and disruptiveness. Combat these thoughts with actions that are the opposite of what you're constantly thinking about. You can do better than anything that has existed in the past.

You don't have to go back to people from your past. You don't have to do anything that you don't want to, so stop choosing to be emotionally messy. You're to blame for what does and doesn't exist in your life. Be Encouraged, your peace is on its way, but it's just waiting for you to stop self-sabotaging your progression.

<u>Cognition 6</u>

"Sometimes your best shot won't make the goal."

There are many life coaches and people who will tell you to never stop trying at something. They will tell you to try and try again. Many will tell you that you should never give up on your goals and your dreams, but I'm not one of those people.

I do believe that you should try your absolute best at accomplishing the goals you have set for yourself, but I'm also of the belief that at some point in your life you have to make a decision to either stay on that path or to move in a new direction. A new direction better suited for you.

It's of utmost importance to know when you've give it your best shot but if I may continue to speak truth to you, that best shot sometimes will not be good enough to place you not only where you would like to be but where you need to be. Now, you can continue to force the goal to work, or you can begin to use your energy in other areas better suited to your talents. Wisdom comes in different forms, but for a fact, wisdom is also knowing when to walk away. That's not quitting; that's courage. To know when enough is enough.

Walking away after giving it the absolute best combined with a detailed plan of action is not the same as quitting in general. Be wise enough to let go and move on so that the next possibility can begin. You're destined for more than one great thing.

Truth is you can do a multitude of things that will be great but without knowing where to put your energy and when, all your hard work could go to waste. Understand that timing is everything, and when you delay in situations not best designed for you, you run the risk of missing the right time for that which is.

Charles Darwin said, "A man who dares to waste one hour of time has not discovered the value of life." What Charles Darwin is suggesting is that your time can never be returned to you so understand that every moment that you spend doing something unfulfilling is literally costing you your life. It can be scary letting go of something, someone or a situation that you've invested time with but moving to the next life experience will benefit you more than you understand.

Truth is, the next experience that you set your energy on has a better chance to teach you what you need to learn in order to make the goal you were unable to complete in the past become completed in the present. That's called progression, staying where you were with no new movement is called stagnation. Which do you desire? Progression or stagnation? Staying flat or elevation? You know what you want, so make the change.

I'm sure you can look around at some of your friends, family, and associates and see people who need to move on from where they are but they remain even when every bone and muscle in their body is hurting. Their spiritual energy is miserable, depressing and suffocating but they don't want to move on because their goal was to be whatever it is or was in that situation. They're potentially missing out on many blessings by remaining focused on where they don't need to be. That's part frustration and part stubbornness, and they are blocking their own dreams from being accomplished.

If any of this sounds familiar to you, then I'm speaking about you as well. Formulate a new plan for the next goal you have for yourself and begin working on it and then begin stepping on it. Spend another hour if you must on where you are but don't spend a lifetime there.

Cognition 7

"The Truth about the law of attraction? It's not just speaking it into existence, it's also doing it into existence. Be your attraction."

There are many theories that exist in this world that teaches you that everything and anything you speak and think from within your being and out into the universe that those same thoughts will come back into your life.

They warn you to be careful with your tongue and your mind because if you aren't ready for what you ask for you may mess it up when it arrives. These teaching will even warn you that simply thinking about the things you don't want will also bring it into your life.

Noesis

These teachings will never mention the word fear, but the fact is that "warning" you is a form of fear placed thinking and it's another way to keep you thinking that there is a consequence from God or the universe simply because of your thinking. In these philosophies, it is equivalent to the religious view of sinning, but it will never be called that because they understand the only sin is in not living.

Let these words resonate within your core, there are no punishments from God and the Universe so live free and think freer! Controversial words I know but the only punishment that rains down are the shackles you place around your life.

If you must fear something fear that, because the reality is that thinking and speaking by itself is never enough to bring things into your life. You can think and say whatever you want without worrying about attracting these things into your life.

Are there consequences that come about because of your thinking? Sure there are consequences for positive thinking and negative thinking, e.g., feel better emotionally and spiritually, but your negative thinking will require negative actions that brings more negativity into your life. The reason people tend to believe that it's their thinking that is attracting certain things into their life is because it's hard for positive thinking to coalesce with negative actions and vice versa, so people change or adapt to get on the same wavelength. As you know, in many cases, positive and negative are opposite energies that fight against one another but of course in the world of magnetic attraction this is not the case, but in this specific chapter we are speaking of life attractions.

Having positive thinking combined with negative actions is similar to swimming against the current but then immediately turning around to swim with the current and this confliction causes your spirit to be torn.

What happens next is that instead of continuing this struggle you then acquiesce and begin doing actions or thoughts that go hand to hand the easiest. Eventually, your ego convinces you that your negative thinking would be better suited not caring because not caring is easy.

Noesis

As you begin not caring with your thoughts and actions, the negative thinking and negative actions are now operating on the same wavelength and in tandem. The consequences of the said thoughts and actions enter your life at a faster rate. This is how the law of attraction truly works. It's the same with positive thinking and positive actions.

It makes most sense then for you to think positive and be positive because it moves you closer to peace, it moves you forward towards your goals. This is the only way you will attract things into your life faster. It requires you to put in the work first in your mind because if you don't believe it mentally, you will never do any actions that will bring forth the correct actions. It all starts in your mind friend.

For this week, focus on thinking positive. Write down some positive affirmations that you can say each week and then follow up with some positive actions.

Cognition 8

"Your struggle was brought on by your decisions and
so is your success."

This cognition will be a bit touchy for a lot of people
who believe that God or the devil have created
obstacles and situations specifically for you so that you
may grow stronger. As always it's easier to blame
someone else for the struggles that you face and yes
it's true that in some of the circumstances existing in
your life that are there are there much in part of
because of other human beings performing actions
that made it harder for you but it's never hard enough
to stop you in your tracks completely.

The reality is that you yourself on some level have
created what is and what isn't in your life. God is no
putting you through trials and tribulations in order to

make you stronger. If God does exist (and we may never know), then God certainly knows that you're strong enough already. It's completely accurate that you do become stronger if you come out on top of the situation that you created but you don't come out of it because of God just like you don't fail because of God.

The moment you begin taking claim and ownership in your life is also the moment that you take as much control over your life that is possible. In earnest, those closest to you will love you even more for finally acknowledging this area of understanding.

When we think about our family and friends lives I think you would agree that when viewing their life from the outsider's perspective, you can quickly identify what actions they took or are taking that's causing their struggle, am I right?

The key to becoming more adept of your own life is to take just a small percentage of that same perspective and apply it to your own life; because when you do your life improves tenfold.

Noesis

This philosophy can be hard for people to accept because it's easier to want to look elsewhere for what's actually going on in your life. Believe it or not you've been doing this unconsciously for a very long time, and if you're living a religious lifestyle, you most assuredly have been taught to give away your accomplishments to something outside of yourself. Trust me when I say that by doing that gives away the only true power you have over your life. The same can be said for blaming others for your struggles.

This is not to say that God/Universe doesn't help, but the great truth is that you (not anything outside of you) are the cause of what exists in your current moment. It's how you think that attracts what you have or don't have and it's in your actions that determine what stays and what goes.

 If you remember nothing else from this cognition, remember these last words and embed it into your life. We attract all that exists...it is not given it is brought."

Cognition 9

"Tough conversations need to be had with other people but none more important than the tough conversations that you need to have with yourself."

Let me ask you a few questions, and I want you to honestly answer them. Do you think people can afford to live their entire life without ever taking a hard look at themselves? Can you afford to go your entire life without ever having tough love conversations about your very own life? How long are you willing to avoid the conversations that will bring you clarity?

Truth is, not many people can benefit from ignoring tough love conversations but understand that clarity brings progress and with progress comes growth and with growth comes the sense of accomplishment. The flip side of this, of course, is the fact that without that clarity stagnation takes over.

There's a reason why people procrastinate, and that reason is that people become comfortable with where they are in life. Many individuals refuse to have certain conversations because chances are it's going to require them to change something in their life that takes a lot of work to change once they begin the tough love conversations.

Honestly writing; from my spirit to my mind and from my mind to my fingers I'm expressing to all of you that the time is now to stop avoiding both personally and professionally the tough love conversations that need to be had about your life.

Reader, avoidance may have a different definition of fear but make no mistake; they're in the same family tree as they both leave you in a state of staleness and unhappiness. Let me be frank, today I want you to examine your life and begin the conversations that will bring you the change that you seek. It won't be fun, it won't be exhilarating, and it won't be easy, but it will be the best thing you've done for yourself in a

very long time. You may be asking what
conversations am I referring to? I'm speaking of the
conversations that center around why you've been
single for so long, why you're still working the same
job after all these years, why you don't have many
friends, why you're depressed. I'm speaking of any
type of conversation that will bring you out a
situation that you longer desire to be in.

Desire is the key word here because truthfully, most
people will not make changes until they desire to do
so. It's a known fact that they won't have tough
conversations. So formulate a plan and follow through
with the plan until their desire to change outweighs
their discontent. You surely desire freedom right?
You surely desire freedom to be your own person
correct? So go get that freedom, because clarity is just
that, freedom.

Noesis

<u>Cognition 10</u>

"Stop confusing being fearful with waiting on God."

There's a difference between meditating (praying) in an effort of waiting for God to give you a sign before you make a move and being fearful of making a move. It's unfortunate, but many people use God (and if you're uncomfortable with the word God, replace it with universe) as their excuse for not changing the things in their lives that they know they need to.

Maybe you've been using God as an excuse, and that's okay but it's time to stop, it's time to become better, it's time to make moves. Have you ever said "I'm waiting on God" or "I'm waiting on the universe?" I'm sure you have, and if not, I'm sure you've heard this statement due to someone you know or a video you watched of someone uttering the words, "I'm waiting on God."

Let's be frank, living by these words creates a handicap that most people pretend doesn't exist but every day it affects their life. Personally, I've watched and listened to many people go through their entire life "waiting on God" to give them a sign that will give them the strength they need to make a decision about their life and that sign never comes. Ultimately what ends up happening is that person becomes so exhausted of their situation they find the smallest occurrences and choose it as the sign from God that they were waiting on.

Here's a question, could it be possible that the signs were always there but because of fear, they never saw the signs that were directly in front of them? Of course it's possible, and of course, it's true, so have you been missing the signs?

Probably, but it's easy to do when fear is blinding you, paralyzing you from moving and it's easy to miss what exists inside of you when you continue to look outside of yourself for the signs. You are the sign, but you don't fully commit to yourself. Focus on the truth that God has placed everything inside of you to know what your next moves should be. What you have in you is more than enough, but you don't trust yourself enough to make the harder decisions in your life, so you sit and wait for a sign. A sign that may come eventually but only because you'll have a moment of true clarity to see it.

This moment is your moment of clarity. This movement you feel inside is your moment to move forth with the power created inside of you. This moment gives you back the power that you so freely gave away. Get in touch with your senses, get in touch with your spirit and you will stop making excuses as to why you're waiting on God for a sign. In due time you'll go from saying I'm waiting on God to I'm waiting on myself.

Cognition 11

"Anger is so powerful that it convinces you that it's okay to spew hate towards the very people in the same struggle as you."

Anger is a combination of emotions unreleased and feelings unexpressed exploding uncontrollably, and it has no place in the life of the spiritual being attempting to live in peace.

Truth be told (and read these words carefully), anger, if left unattended in its small place, will grow into other areas of your life, and before you know what has happened, you will be identified as a person who has anger issues.

Most people do have some form of anger issue that requires a slight fix, and yes the majority of the people with anger management issues can adopt a new path forward that's opposite of uncontrolled anger.

Do you ever find yourself getting angry and then get even angrier at yourself when you realize you allowed yourself to get so disconnected from the peace within yourself?

When you find yourself in an angry state of being it means that you've allowed someone to control your emotions. This doesn't mean that you can't be frustrated or disappointed in someone and in situations but anger takes you to a place where only the ego benefits.

Who benefits from anger? Not the recipient and certainly not you because most people feel horrible about what was done and said after they've calmed down. If you remember nothing else from this cognition, remember this; anger is the bruised ego's way of convincing itself that it's still in control.

Anger in the sense that I'm speaking of means "hostility," and in that hostile state the person who is angry is yelling, cursing, fighting and/or attempting destroy and demoralize another human being. They will deflect things away from themselves and will play the role of the victim. The angry person or people loses control of all of their emotions except the emotion of anger and will rarely want to hear anything you have to say that is in the opposite of their feelings and point of view. They are right, and you are wrong, or if you are the angry person, you are right, and they are wrong.

This is not the path of inner peace. Peace cannot exist in the same place as anger just as Heaven and Hell cannot exist in the same moment in time. When you find yourself getting angry, ask yourself if that moment is worth the energy and time that you are about to lose.

Ask yourself if the angry words that you're about to allow out of your mouth are worth the hurt you will cause. Ask yourself if there is a better way to express how you're feeling in that moment and if you find the answer to be no, then learn to walk away respectfully until you're able to revisit the situation and conversation in an effective manner.

Noesis

Stay in control of what you can my friend, don't lose control of your emotions and never give anyone power over your emotions. You must learn to let go of the things you can't control, but you can surely control your anger if you so desire but that requires you to be able to identify the emotion beforehand, and it also requires you being able to identify when someone is only adding fuel to the fire. Remember, everyone agreeing with you is not encouraging you for your benefit but rather for theirs.

The person or people your anger is aimed towards are human just like you and they too, are trying to navigate the failed system that taught them little to nothing about effectively communicating and understanding the emotional sides of life. Understand this, you're in this together even if it doesn't feel like it.

Cognition 12

"Half of your problems are a direct result of ignoring problem number one."

Problems come, and problems go, but there seems to always be a few problems that remain no matter what other solutions you create to eliminate some of the situations that exist in your life. Why is that? Well, it often happens because of two main reasons, and those reasons are, one, assuming it will just go away and two, re-opening the door to the problem.

The truth is (and I'm sure you know this) human beings aren't immune to problems, and no matter how well you plan your life there will always be something that will try to throw a wrench in those well-made plans.

Noesis

It happens, and it's very easy to try to ignore the problem with the hope that the problems you're faced with will simply disappear, but they won't. Let me be frank, problems just don't disappear without some form of action being taken by someone, somewhere that dissolves the problem.

Most of the problems that people are faced with wouldn't have to exist if they tackled problem number one in the very beginning. Let's say for example that you don't understand how credit works but yet you get a credit card anyway, and you then max out your credit card.

Hypothetically speaking there would now be a few problems right? Well, what's problem number one? Problem number one is that you don't know how credit works. The solution is to get educated on how credit works before you do anything else. This will help stop the other problems that have now surfaced because of your choice to not be educated in the credit world.

Let's say you keep finding yourself intimately involved with a person who doesn't respect you or your time. You know that it's not a healthy relationship, but yet you never leave or worse yet, you leave and come back. What's problem number one? Figuring out the why and fixing the broken mental pieces of your mind.

Your reoccurring problems are your Achilles heel, but your problems only remain because mentally you haven't hit rock bottom when it comes to those particular troublesome situations. It's hard to admit, but you have yet to convince yourself that serious change is needed.

 You believe that you still have time to fix the problem that remains, but the truth is that by delaying the inevitable you allow other problems to stack on top of problem number one and you end up spending time trying to fix those problems first while the catalyst of your problems goes untouched. Haven't you had enough?

You don't have to hit rock bottom before you make the change to eliminate problem number one. In fact, you'll be much better off by identifying it, coming up with a solution and then applying the solution consistently until it no longer exists and until you no longer desire going back to the old ways. Half of your problems exist, yes, because of ignoring problem number one but half your problems can cease to exist by paying attention to it.

Cognition 13

"At some point in your life, you have to get tired of the stagnation. You have to finally decide to stop making decisions for yourself that are based upon how someone else will feel."

I saw a friend of mine come to the realization that she had been living her entire life based on the perception of what others may think and she immediately began to cry when discussing her situation to me. As I explained to her, the tears that were coming down her face were tears of change. She was finally aware of her past choices and actions, and it hurt her deeply because she felt she wasted too many years and made too many wrong mistakes.

As I mentioned to her those tears should be enough to stimulate a new pattern if change is truly desired.

Your tears, your sleepless nights should be enough to conjure up change, but at some point you have to decide to stop going around in the very circles you created decades ago. Human beings do the same thing over and over again with the same pattern each and every year at the same time and even with the same person or people. I call it the pattern of recycled emotions.

Instead of creating new thought processes that move them forward, most people who are stuck in particular situations are making decisions for their life based on what they felt from the past, a recycled emotion.

For better or for worse they're unconsciously remembering emotions, feelings, and memories from the past that were tied to people who were in their life previously or the present now. The recycled emotion reminds them of how they felt when someone other than themselves was disappointed or happy with a decision that they made and they hesitate.

Noesis

What's happening is that they remember those emotions and feelings and before you make a new decision that will dramatically change your life for the better you begin to ask, "What will my mom think"? What would my dad think"? "What would my friends think?" "What will my partner think"? "What will my family think and what will my church family think if I make this decision?"

The facts are that many questions get asked, but they often forget to ask the one fundamental question. What will they themselves think and they often never ask that question at all. They place the self, last, when it needs to be the first question and the last question.

Highlight this next sentence; you only get one life to live that we know of, so stop making choices for your life based on your recycled emotions. The next major decision that you make for your life, make it fully on what's best for you and you only, everyone else will align with you or realign with someone else who's not part of your life, and this will release the energy that was stagnant and will open up space for new positive energy to enter.

This is part of the beginning of inner peace and that's how you begin to find your true voice.

Cognition 14

"Weaknesses are strengths that you haven't learned to master."

A lifetime sounds like a long time but as we soon find out through living, life goes by quicker than the changing seasons, but if there's one thing that all humans are destined to experience in this lifetime, it's struggles.

No matter how long or how short you live the struggles come and the struggles go. Financial struggles, emotional struggles, romantic struggles, weight struggles and so on. Understand me, if you haven't struggled yet then know your struggle is coming.

This is not me being the bearer of bad news, no, this is me giving you the cold hard truth. You'll struggle with many things during your lifetime and some of these struggles you may never understand as well as the next man or woman but as long as you learn to understand them the best that you can then you can always call that progress.

Most of the struggles that you'll end up experiencing will come due to the fact that you're not strong in that area of expertise. Some will call these struggles weaknesses, and for the most part, it's true, they are weaknesses, but they don't make you weak. Let's understand that point.

Weaknesses don't make you weak they just make you human. So if you don't know how to build your credit that doesn't make you weak that makes you human. If you don't know how to communicate effectively, that doesn't make you weak, that makes you human. If you don't know how to love a man o woman properly, that doesn't make you weak, that makes you human!

Do you know what else makes you human? Weaknesses! The God honest truth is that weaknesse are strengths that you haven't learned to master and without knowing where you're weak you can't truly know where you're strong. Weaknesses are also your opportunities to make them a strength of yours if you're willing to put in the work to understand them. Like many things in life you'll always have an opportunity to become a master in area's that you don't understand.

Think about your life and ask yourself how your strengths came to be. Some of your strengths came naturally but most of them you had to work at over and over again. You had to practice on them for years, or you had to read/study materials in order to become a master of it.

 Listen, you have the ability to turn any weakness into a strength if you truly desire it to be so. Let you remember that God represents strength, and you came from within God, so unless you believe God to be weak then there is no weakness in you, it's just traits adopted from one human to another that can easily be broken.

Remember these last few lines and take them to your grave. No human whether it be man or woman gets to determine your true strength or weakness. The definer is always the creator of the mindset.

Cognition 15

"Make your present as nostalgic as you remember
your past to be."

Honesty is best served with love, so with love let you
be honest with yourself in regards to this next
question. How does your present moment compare
to your past memories? Better, equal or worse? The
Good old days always seem better as you think back
on them in comparison to your present moment.

Naturally, you think about all the good feelings you
had flowing back then and reminisce for hours about
what things were like in your yesteryears and
sometimes wondering how you can get that back.

Those thoughts conjure up good energy for people,
and rightfully so, those moments were precious for
you and them, but people tend to always leave out

the complications they had back then when they reminisce. The truth is, it can be uncomfortable remembering the bad because most people don't want to ever feel that way ever again and fear that thinking about the bad will open up new opportunities for the bad to now exist in their present moment.

The fact is, people don't like to remember the bad days, the bad things and the bad moments so when they think about their past they only like to remember all the good that was. It's easy to forget the bad, especially when in comparison to your present moment.

The present moment is always better than the past moment because it is what it was and the present will always be what is which is a beautiful thing. It can be difficult however because in the present moment you're still living in both the good and the bad but how do you begin making your present moment as nostalgic as your past?

First, you need to acknowledge all the good things that's happening for you in the present moment and to remember that things could always be worse than they are. Secondly, when you think about the past, ask yourself what were you doing then that made you feel so happy? Then ask yourself if you're doing those things now. And if you aren't, ask yourself one last question. Why aren't you? No really, why aren't you?

Why aren't you doing what you really want to do today? Is there a legitimate reason preventing you from enjoying the present? And when I say legitimate, I mean an actual reason that doesn't allow you to go enjoy the journey.

Ralph Waldo Emerson said, "Life is a journey, not a destination," and if you aren't enjoying your journey, it's no wonder you dislike your current destination. Live my friend like your life depends on it. Make your present-day moments so memorable that when you look back on it years from now, you'll still be happy you did.

Don't live solely in the unpleasant moments because in truth they're just there to help remind you of all the good that you do have. This isn't hyperbole. Everything in life has a balance to it. How can you remember to enjoy the good if you don't ever have a reminder of how quick it can be gone? Unfortunate situations that pop up don't have to take away from your fortunate situations. Get back to living and enjoying the moments you have because you truly don't know when it will be your last. May this chapter remind you to go live fiercely, fierily, and fantastically.

Cognition 16

"One day you'll have to go to war with false self to allow authentic self to live without turmoil."

There are at least two different you's inside of the one you. The you that was created by others (that you adopted) and the you that is waiting for you to create (that you never knew). The true you is the authentic you, but getting to that you requires breaking from traditions, thoughts, beliefs, and actions that you believe at your very core is the authentic you. It's uneasy, uncomfortable, and sometimes in some circles unacceptable. This I promise you, it will never be unfulfilling.

Let me operate in complete transparency with these next few words, you'll have to be a little audacious to go against everything that has been taught to you, but when you understand that your life depends on winning this war, you'll do everything in your power to be victorious. Why? Because you're going to reach a point in your life where you're no longer truly happy with certain aspects of your life

. You're going to come to a point where you'll want some major changes to happen and the only way that you'll be able to truly find the change you need will be to break free from it all. That's scary, but sometimes you must break apart the pieces to be able to understand the reassembling of it all.

Sun Tzu stated in his book The Art of War that, "All warfare is deception," and unbeknownst to you, you've been in a world war and the ones leading the deception have been easily winning. This particular world war is not being fought with military machines but instead; it's being fought with military-like expertise against you.

This war that you're in includes but not limited to your spirituality, your mental stability, your financial capabilities, and your ability to understand self-image and none of these things should be decided by anyone else except you.

But who are you? What is the deception? How can you win a war if you don't know where to begin? This is what you do, and this too is where it always begins. Everything begins and ends with you. You begin with you! Who you want to be, who you don't want to be, what you think is important and how you view life must begin with you and things must end with you and everything else in-between should be the things that you truly believe in and want to be known for.

No one outside of you gets to define you; not now, not ever. The thing is, your life up until this point (or maybe a few years ago) was defined by others. Your self-image, your spiritual practice, your idea of what love is and what success is has been defined by others.

I implore you to be a free thinker and to be more in tune with true human connections. I also suggest that whatever it is that you're unsatisfied with in your life or mind that you challenge it! Even if it's the simplest characteristic that you no longer want to be associated with. Challenge it!

Ask why it exists and if it needs to be changed. Are you tired of having trust issues? Challenge it! Are you tired of self-sabotaging your life? Challenge it and then change it! Go to war with all the discrepancies in your life that need to be corrected. Fight for your life passionately and precisely.

If you're unable to deconstruct the false you then you must get the help of someone not named you and when they give you constructive criticism be open to the words they say. Ask those closest to you for the God honest truth. Analyze it, challenge it and if the shoe fits, accept it as such and if you don't want to be that way, change it.

It's time to change the narrative of your life. It's time to take control of your life. For way too long you gave someone else the pen to write your life story, and you've been living it the best way that you could. You've believed that you are who they say you are and believe it or not, there is an authentic you waiting to be alive and guess what? You deserve it; discover it and live it. Good luck!

<u>Cognition 17</u>

"God never left you or casted you out of which you came, but you've been taught that you were born into less than when in fact you're more than what you can possibly imagine."

People have been misled to believe that they've fallen from God's grace. This thought process creates in you the desire to prove yourself from the very beginning of your consciousness. You're good enough. Matter of fact you're more than good enough; you're God enough, but unfortunately, when you've been taught that you aren't good enough from that which you came you spend most your adult life trying to make up for something that you already had, acceptance.

So let's begin to end the negative viewpoint right now by re-affirming that you never fell from God's grace; which means you were good enough to stay connected to whatever that is God. And as I mentioned in The Unbelievable Truth: A Guide to Finding Peace, God is whatever you need God to be. Let's move on.

When you think about the concept of losing acceptance from the creator, you unconsciously live like you have something to prove. You're taught that you weren't good enough from the very moment you exited your mother's womb if you live in a religious home.

The argument can be made that those born into an Atheist home have the jump on everyone else when it comes to understanding self. For they only have their parents/caregiver to blame while others have their parents and God.

Let's use the example of your parents for a moment in trying to understand the unacceptance theory of God and you. If your parents casted you out or told you that you're no longer in their good graces, you would ask them the question of why? You would ask, "What did I do to no longer be loved by you?" And if we are to answer truthfully, you would likely feel less than for a certain amount of time because most of us want nothing more in life than to make our parents proud of us.

In human terms, God (for whatever God is) is the ultimate parent, the ultimate creator and if you throw out all the human-made reasoning for not being good enough for God (remember you were told you were casted out), we can then ask the question. Why would you no longer be in the good grace of God?

What could you have possibly done at the moment of your birth except be born? Is being born the ultimate displeasure to God? If so, why let humans be born, to begin with? Many will tell you that you're paying the price for past human actions.

Well, unless you believe God to be a God to hold a serious grudge (we're talking millenniums) then punishing future generations for past generations that they never even knew makes for one cold-hearted God.

Noesis

It's important to remember that you're the walking, living image of your parents combined. You cannot not be what they are because what they are is literally what allows you to exist. No matter how much you may want to be disconnected from them, the cells in your body won't allow it. What we know exist in the Heavens above us, we also know that it exists in us as well. Theory has it that God is Heaven and in us exist carbon, nitrogen and oxygen atoms in our bodies, as well as atoms of all other heavy elements. These ingredients existed in previous generations of stars 4.5 billion years ago.

Astrophysicist Carl Sagan said "The cosmos is within us. We are made of star-stuff. We are a way for the universe to know itself." As if that wasn't enough evidence, Astrophysicist Neil Degrasse Tyson said "The atoms of our bodies are traceable to stars that manufactured them in their cores and exploded these enriched ingredients across our galaxy, billions of years ago.

For this reason, we are biologically connected to every other living thing in the world. We are chemically connected to all molecules on Earth. And we are atomically connected to all atoms in the universe. We are not figuratively, but literally stardust."

Therefore you're still connected to God because it's impossible to not be what makes you what you are, and if you weren't good enough at birth, then that means God was not good enough either. So understand that there is nothing you need to do to prove your worth. There is nothing that you need to do to create favor for God.

You're an amazing human being who just needs to trust more in yourself and who needs to do away with the image of needing approval. If God is good enough (which God is) then so are you. Live your life as the God that you are (more on this in another cognition) and you'll live a life truly fulfilled.

Noesis

Cognition 18

"You can live your entire life believing in beliefs.
Defining yourself by concepts that are true and
untrue, but there is only one belief lived by you that
you can truly call real and that's the belief in
yourself."

Depletion is the catalyst of frustration, and without
replenishing what's being extracted, it can lead to
breakdowns mentally and spiritually. So let me ask
you, how often are you building yourself up? How
much time do you spend uplifting your mind, body,
and soul?

How much energy do you spend believing in others
but not giving that same amount of belief in self? If
you answer those questions with 'I don't know," then
trust me when I say you aren't giving yourself enough
of you. You've probably made many decisions in
your life based on the belief of who you say you are.

Noesis

Let me give you a few examples to drive this point home. A few examples are, "I believe I'm a caring person, so I always try to care for others." I believe I'm a nurturer, so I always try to fix things in people that are broken." "I believe I'm an extrovert, so I always go out and have fun when my friends ask me." "I'm a Muslim, and I believe it's right to only live by what the Quran says."

It's very easy to get caught up in the concepts of who you define as yourself, and there's nothing wrong with these concepts but never believe more in them than in yourself; for at your core, your spiritual energy needs the most attention.

Your soul is who you are, do you believe your soul? No, I'm not asking if you believe your soul to be real, I'm asking do you believe in yourself? YOU ARE SOUL, so if you don't believe in self, what do you believe in? If you do, then go forth in life replenishing your soul with things that make it severely stronger and magnificently connected. Believe in you more than any other concept that you define as you. Be unapologetic about strengthening that which you are.

Noesis

When you begin to feel lost, when your mind begins to feel foggy and your spirit begins to feel disconnected, pull back to balance and away from anything and everything that isn't directly linked to replenishing your soul.

When you do this, there is nothing that can stop you except yourself. When you do this, the power is literally in your control. Remember, that you're the one thing in your life that is truly real. Without you, there can be no other concepts to adopt, and there can be no other beliefs in your life that take away from you.

While the possibility may exist that you can't get anything without first giving, it's absolutely true that you can't give what you don't have. Never stop believing in soul and you will always believe in you, and I promise you'll always be happier too.

Cognition 19

"The future now is fluid, and like liquid, it spills in many different directions when spilled on the table."

Sometimes in life, you need to be willing to spill you cup so that you can see which direction you'd like to go. Imagine for a second that the cup is your body and the liquid inside the cup is your soul and while your soul can be perfectly happy staying inside the cup it's true expression doesn't come until it's able to see all the options that exist and not only seeing what exist but also being able to choose one of those many options for itself.

No soul truly loves feeling confined, and while our souls may be confined to our physical bodies, our spirits are happier after our time on earth has passed.

Noesis

Our bodies are the cup, and our spirits are the liquid stuck in the current state that it must exist in.

You see, living inside that cup, your soul understands that other life options exist outside the walls of that cup, but it doesn't know what those options are in its entirety because it can't see the path of those options completely.

It's view of what if is blocked by obstacles we've created in life. It only gets a glimpse of those options when there is the occasional spillage, when the cup occasionally spills over the edge. That occasional glimpse happens in most cases when we're sad, tired of a situation, and/or restless and we feel change is needed.

So, we begin to google search different life options other than the one we currently live in. The good news is that there are many paths that your life can go but not if you don't allow your soul to spill out into the world. What will your future now be? Will it be living in the existence of what your current now is?

Noesis

Are you going to set your soul free or will your future now be dictated by everything prior to this moment? If there's nothing wrong with your current now, then do your very best to carry what you have now into the future and fight for your life to maintain it. But if for some reason there are parts of your current now that you'd like to change then change you must because the possibilities of what your life can be are infinite and you deserve to enjoy at least one of those many possibilities.

This requires sacrifice, this requires faith in self, and it requires taking a leap that's so downright scary that you'll think it's better to remain where you are. But how boring would life be if you never took any risk based on the faith you have in yourself?

I have faith in you because I know you're made of the same ingredients that have made me, and I know my many possibilities because I've tipped over my cup and set my soul free. Don't let all that you currently know be all that you ever knew. The free souls are waiting on you to spill over your cup.

<u>Cognition 20</u>

"Facts will never matter to the people who believe
their beliefs are indeed facts."

Many wars have begun because people disagree on
their beliefs, many relationships have ended because
someone felt passionately about their belief, and
complete strangers have become family because their
beliefs brought them together.

Throughout your life, there will be people who you'll
find on your many paths that will try to convince you
that their belief is more important than yours. Even
worse, some of them will try to convince you that
their belief is indeed the right way to be and that
yours is the wrong way. Listen to me; there is no
wrong or right way there are just ways to proceed
forward.

Noesis

Beliefs are not facts, not yours, not theirs and not even mine. Beliefs are the thought processes that people adopted to help them understand how to fit in. Most beliefs are just ways for people to feel most comfortable in the world they live in.

Beliefs are also mostly thought processes that have been taught by one person and passed down from one person to another. Understand that there are very few original beliefs that people are living by and there's nothing wrong with that.

What's unfortunate however is when people with non-flexible beliefs cause turmoil in human relationships because they don't want to listen to facts. Belief over facts should never be a thing, and you should never let your belief overrule the facts presented. Facts matter and so do your beliefs, but your beliefs should never cause division, turmoil, and angst in relationships.

Let your beliefs lead you down positive moral roads but let the facts lead you down the logical roadways that brings all ethnicities together. Use your intellect to progress you further and then let your beliefs keep you focused on the bigger plan.

Trust in the next words of this paragraph. Don't become the person who doesn't know when to set aside their beliefs to better the relationship, to better the situation or to better the world.

Don't become the person who's too stubborn to listen to both sides of the isles and don't become so ingrained in your beliefs that it causes friction between people. There's no such thing as proven beliefs because once your beliefs become proven, they are then facts, and if it's a fact, it can't be a belief so enrich yourself with proven facts and learn to live in a world where both your belief and the facts can exist without cognitive dissonance.

<u>Cognition 21</u>

"If only I could remain as free as a child I'd be able to question everything and conquer the world in the same breath."

Children can be fearless, so fearless in fact that they don't care about the dangers that exist on the other side of their desired goal. The fact of the matter is that sometimes most children are able to think freer and be freer than adults. They have no fear; at least not until it's taught to them. They say " I want to climb this tree" and they either do or at least try.

If they're unable to climb the tree they easily move on; in their minds, they don't see the fear of falling or the failure of not being able to. They see nothing and feel nothing but the excitement of the attempt and then it's on to the next grandest idea. This is our natural state of being, fearlessly living with no regrets, living in the moment, and moving on to the next life experience without fear.

As adults, we understand that every tree doesn't have to be climbed and that every idea doesn't have to be pursued because we understand that sometimes the risk is not worth the reward. However, adults can often over think the things they desire most.

I know too many people who are more paralyzed by just the thought of failing than they are anything else and that's no way to live. You and everyone else are fierce individuals who are designed to do fierce things, so it's time for people to get back to fiercely living.

What are you most afraid of? Finding your happiness or the feeling of not making your dreams reality? Here's a wild thought; most people aren't afraid of failure because most people have failed their entire life; they know failure, and they aren't afraid of it because they know how to handle it.

These same people are more afraid of success because they don't know what to do once they achieve it and they aren't sure how to keep it once they have it. They are more afraid of success than they are of failure. Isn't that crazy? The tree to your success can be right in front of you, and all most people will do is look at it and walk away.

I don't want that to be you; I desire so much more for you, so what keeps you stagnant from climbing the tree you really want to climb; other people or yourself? The universe that we exist in allows all people to be who they want, do what they want and live how they want, it allows you to do anything that your mind can create.

The universe we exist in also accepts the action of doing nothing or continuing to do what you currently are but you and I know that there's something that you'd like to do differently in your life, but you look at the height of the tree and think "it's just too dangerous to climb that high up."

Find your inner child and dream like you never dreamt before. Do it before it's too late, do it before you look back at your life and regret not doing more, not living more and not being fearless more and fearful less. Retrain your brain to see the world through the eyes of a child. A world where they don't see the color of someone's skin, a world where they don't allow beliefs to separate them from the people they don't know and in a world that allows you to live in the moment. This is you, this is me, this is us; so let's be these things collectively.

So, I ask you, What's the next tree you want to climb?

<u>Cognition 22</u>

"Pain, disappointment, and sorrow are the ingredient
for understanding self."

People hide their tears and hold in their pain for fear
of being seen as weak but what if I told you that true
strength is allowing those tears and pain to be seen
and released? What if I told you that all energy that
enters your body will at some point be released from
your body?

These sound like hypothetical questions but in these
questions is also the truth, and it's damaging to your
soul to pretend that you always have it all together,
it's not beneficial to put forth a fake smile when the
hurt is outweighing the joy.

When you need to cry you need to cry; not try to act
tough, when you need scream in frustration scream

Noesis

frustration; not tell people you're okay. You aren't meant to hide your emotions, allow them to be set free and shown. I learned at a very young age that there's strength in being able to balance the range of emotions we have but that there is also strength in the release of them all in a healthy manner. We're spiritual beings experiencing human lives, and part of being human is our emotions. Why then would you want to suppress the emotions that are you in this physical form?

All energy is not created equal, and the same can be said about the type of energy that we release from our body. What we take in isn't always the energy we put out, and sometimes we take in very little positive energy and often release that energy by giving it to other people, only leaving the negative energy to remain inside of us.

All the energy that enters your spiritual bodies don't always get discharged and sometimes when you do discharge some of that energy you release it in a manner that does more harm to you; causing more negative energy to re-enter into your body, mind and soul because what you give out is what you get back, thus creating a recycling pattern of negative energy.

When people experience pain, disappointment, and sorrow it gives them the opportunity to examine their deepest feelings, emotions, and thoughts because in their darkest times they're focused on the why. Why do I feel this way? Why would they do that to me? Why did I do that?

When you experience these feelings, it gives you the opportunity to learn yourself, examine yourself and to build a stronger, smarter more balanced you, and that's ultimately the most important thing during your time on earth; building a better you.

It's important to remember that the energy equated with pain and sorrow does have the ability to be flipped into peace and happiness, but people can't turn that energy from one to the other without first being able to process the energy they're feeling at first.

To turn that negative energy into positive energy one must deconstruct the negative energy to reconstruct

Noesis

it; then and only then will you be able to reap the rewards of the positive energy that can change your life.

Learn to allow the energy of pain, sorrow, and disappointment to be released the very first moments you feel those in your life but don't allow those energies to continue. Release it, deconstruct it and construct your new path forward.

I don't think there's any coincidence that some of the greatest songs, movies, books, paintings, and poetry had come when the creators of those projects were dealing with pain in their lives. It's in those darkest times that we see much clearer and can give birth to beautiful things that change the world. Don't be afraid of your emotions, in fact, embrace them, understand them but just don't be consumed by them.

Cognition 23

"If your words can't speak as clear as your actions
then your actions won't be heard."

How much stronger would our relationships be if we
can learn to make our words and actions speak at the
same decibel; to make them be heard at the deepest
and quietest levels is the ultimate spiritual balance tha
exists.

When things fall apart in our relationships we can
listen to what others say is the truth or we can listen
for ourselves and decide why things either fall
together or fall apart. Unbelievably words are never
enough by itself, and even though words can build a
bond, it's the mixture of action and words that make
relationships durable.

Noesis

I remember as a young boy always telling my mom that I loved her and as I got older I began to say it less and less. It wasn't because I didn't love my mom, it was because I just figured she already knew. Then one day my mom asked me "baby, why don't you ever tell me you love me?" and I said, "momma, I don't know, but you know I do." And she said, "son, even though I know you love me, I still need to hear it." From that day on, even until this day, when I am about to finish the conversation with my mom I say "I love you," and I do my very best to also show her that I love her.

Imagine reader, if we can learn to combine both our actions and our words into a smooth melody, we'll then be able to move souls for eternity and build relationships harmoniously. The individual that can seamlessly use both words and actions are soul movers.

Soul movers are aligned with their authentic self and when they give another spiritual being true words with true actions, the spiritual being that's on the receiving end of that authentic alignment can't help but be moved spiritually towards a deeper connection with the soul mover and ultimately feel better about their position not only in your life but in the world.

Don't you want to be a soul mover? The God in you deserves alignment, and I encourage you to practice aligning your words and actions even when it's uncomfortable. I also encourage you to not always rely on someone's action solely. It's true that what people do speaks volumes but remember it's not always loudest. Require people to give the God in you alignment if they want to be in your life.

If you want to be better at relationships (intimate and non-intimate), you must work on making sure your words and your actions align as perfect as you can get them each waking moment. And while there is no such thing as perfect (except possibly the universe) trying to reach for it in this situation can be beneficial for all parties involved.

There's a saying that with practice I'd like you to remove from your life and it's "Talk is cheap." Truthfully talk isn't cheap; in fact, if it does appear as cheap it's likely when the actions don't back the words. However, guess what? Actions are cheap if th words don't back it too. Words are surely valuable for the individuals who need words of affirmation in their relationships and vice versa in regarding actions.

So, I ask you, are actions always a better indicator for care and love? Clearly, it's not. But you can't overlook actions any more than you can words. Both are powerful indicators of positive energy as well as negative energy and together they can be powerful reinforcements for making a cloudy situation clear.

How much damage do humans do with the words that go unsaid? How much damage do humans do with the words that are said the incorrect way?

From this moment on, begin practicing alignment of your words and actions and make no mistake; it won't be easy to break century-old habits but trust in yourself that you can break those old habits. All of your relationships deserve this version of you, but more importantly, you deserve the new you.

<u>Cognition 24</u>

"The toughest pill you'll have to swallow is the belief in the worthiness of yourself. No matter how hard it gets in the different aspects of your life you must be your biggest champion, cheerer, and supporter."

In life people will disappoint you, hurt you and make you lose faith in humanity at times. During these difficult times, it's important to remember that people are flawed. Being flawed is part of what people are; that much is true and this truth includes yourself, and at the end of the day it's unavoidable.

Human beings are designed to make mistakes and caught in the aftermath of those mistakes are often the people who love that mistake-prone person. They hurt us, I hurt others, you hurt others, we hurt others and sometimes the ones we love the most hurt us the most and don't support us in our time of need.

There will be people who don't cheer for you, who don't believe in you and don't support the dreams, desires, and designs that you're trying to give birth to the world. This fact can be heartbreaking but never should it be spirit-breaking because if you believe in your God-self, there should be nothing that breaks you completely.

In a perfect world, you'll always have the deepest, strongest, and wisest support system in your life but as you know we live in a far from perfect world and chances are you will have to be the only support system you have at moments in your life.

So, if you don't know how to support yourself; learn; if you've never cheered for yourself; begin; and if you've never seen yourself as a champion, start. You not being able to do these three things for yourself needs to be non-negotiable in your life; because without you being able to do them, you put your entire identity of self in the hands of someone else and that is always a recipe for complete disaster and you, dear reader, are not destined for disaster but instead greatness.

Your foundation needs to be built on everything that is you. You must be your base so that when the other parts of your life potentially fall apart (they will) and disappoint you, you'll always have you there to save you. Yes, there will be times where even you disappoint you, but the recovery from your own misunderstanding is quicker than the recovery of trying to understand other people's misunderstandings. It makes most sense then that the quicker you recover, the quicker you can get back on your path.

This is not to say that you can't rely on others to help you out of your funks but it is to say that you shouldn't rely on them to pull you out of your funks all the time; because ultimately; most people don't believe it's their responsibility to do so.

Every now and then you do come across individuals who see their friend and family hurting, and they extend their hand, but unfortunately, that's the exception and not the rule.

Noesis

How worthy do you believe yourself to be? What level of Godness do you exist in? That's the real question that needs to be answered. When you look in the mirror how worthy do you see yourself as? God knows how valuable you are to everything in this universe, but God won't stop you from not believing in yourself. God won't stop you from not being your biggest cheerer because that takes away all the power that God gave you, to begin with. God won't stop you from not seeing the God in you because it's up to you to realize who you are, the power you have and that power can't be extinguished unless you allow it to be.

So no matter how low things seem to be, no matter how much you may currently be struggling or how long you've been struggling, if you truly believe in yourself, if you're truly your biggest supporter and stay forever in your corner even when the tears are streaming down your face, you will overcome. Champions are overcomers, and you're a mother-fucking champion.

<u>Cognition 25</u>

"Inner peace can never be interrupted by others, but that won't stop them from trying to give you a glimpse of hell."

Joy, balance, and peace are contagious, and people who become aware of that trinity in your life can attempt to take it away from you. Some people maliciously do this while others unconsciously do this and in both cases, it's up to you to be aware of it.

The reality is, some people are evil and want to take your joy, and some people are good and just want part of what you have because they desire those things as well and think that some of what you have will rub off on their life.

The responsibility falls on you to determine who's worthy of giving some of your peace to and who's

Noesis

not. It's up to you to determine how much you can give without creating a void in your energy field. If you haven't mastered impenetrable peace then you can't spiritually afford to give away pieces of your peace because here's the thing, peace is not something that comes and goes; it's a lifestyle that remains true no matter what's going on around you. You either have it, or you don't and if you almost have it, giving part of what you have away before you've sustained its wholeness for yourself is retrogressing.

Still, it's important to remember that no matter how much peace you believe you have, the good rule of thumb to remember is that someone else wants what you have. Or at the very least want you to be as miserable as them and people will attempt to steal your peace in different ways, deceitful ways and demeaning ways. The most obvious way is by trying to force their personal beliefs on to you or by making you feel wrong about what your personal lifestyle.

Obviously, not all beliefs are bad beliefs, and some beliefs should be adopted but make no mistake reader, don't accept any belief into your spirit that you don't agree one hundred percent with. Peace remains when there are no conflicts existing within your belief system and more importantly inside of you.

I learned in life that the key to living a life of consistent peace, one must stop living by the beliefs of others before us. In fact, I've learned that to find that consistent peacefulness faster, we must live by our own beliefs and rules, we must never fail to challenge our own belief and rules, and we must never be afraid to step outside of beliefs and rules we've established for ourselves in order to continue to evolve.

If at any point in your existence you identify a conflict in your spiritual beliefs or are faced with new evidence that contradicts your beliefs don't turn a deaf ear to it. You'll always owe it to yourself to adapt, to be moldable and to be willing to change to remain at peace with self.

You'll always owe it to yourself to invest in the understanding of new information that can push you closer to Christ consciousness. If you take nothing else from this chapter, then take this. Don't be a victim to your own cognitive dissonance.

Noesis

At the same time and more importantly, don't allow the cognitive dissonance of other people to create unwanted, undesired, and unnecessary discomfort in your life. If misguided, unhappy, and close-minded individuals have the opportunity to rain on your happiness, then they will.

Because the reality of life is that people are rarely fans of what they don't understand and if what you believe, live and breathe causes discomfort for them then they won't be fans of yours because they don't understand you and will have very little desire to do so.

Own your happiness, own your peace and own your life. Don't just march to the beat of your own drum; no, make the drum that creates your sound and let other people figure out how to learn it.

Cognition 26

"Their whispers aren't your truth but what you say to yourself will be the difference between your truth, your greatness and your destiny."

Those who don't know you don't get you and those who don't get you are likely strangers living vicariously through you. They're strangers to knowing who you are, what you're about and how you're trying to live your life and I can say this with absolute confidence because anyone who's a true friend of yours or someone whose opinion you value will know exactly the type of person you are.

Strangers who know not who you are should have very little impact (if any at all) on how you feel about yourself, but sometimes the words of others that you hear through the grapevine can cut deep if you allow it.

The unfortunate truth about people is that when you keep your business and lifestyle private to everyone except those in your circle/family then those on the outside are forced to create their own story-line about who you are, what you do and how you think. They take the little bit that they do know, the little they did know and combine it with the whispers from strangers to build their own version of you to fit the narrative they have of you.

This is most often created in a way to make themselves feel elevated above you because who you appear to be makes them uncomfortable and the only way to feel comfortable again is to create a version of you that's opposite of their own beliefs and lifestyle. Nine times out of ten, the version of you that exists in their mind is slightly negative in one way or another. It's not right, it's not fair but such is life, this is what outsiders do.

Truthfully, sometimes people who were once in your circle and are now in new circles but still interact with parts of your circle contribute to the false narrative as well because they assume they still know you and it's only natural to be bothered by what you've heard them say when you catch wind of it. Most often your first few thoughts are; "*how could they say that*" and "*they know that's not me*" or quite simply it makes you feel "some type of way" about it.

I'm here to tell you that their thoughts, opinions and false narrative about who you are don't matter (insert hand claps)..point….blank….period. They don't matter, and they're on the outside looking in for many reasons, and the only way they can get inside o you is by you allowing them in. Do you choose to give them control over you? Are you going to allow the God in them to have control over the God in you?

I've been there before; I've been the person trying to convince people who don't know me to understand me. I've been the person trying to keep people on th inside who deserve to be on the outside. I've been th person who's caught wind of the whispers of strange and let it affect me. I've been the person on the receiving end of a text message from someone you once called a friend and being in shock from what you just read wanting to go the fuck off on them.

Listen, it's not worth your time, it's not worth your frustration and it's certainly not worth the high blood pressure that's associated with the bullshit that comes along with trying to fix it. Socrates once said, "Strong minds discuss ideas, average minds discuss events, weak minds discuss people," so unless you think Socrates is an idiot, why would you want to waste your time with weak-minded people who just want to discuss what they think they know about your character?

Let the whispers that you hear from strangers fall on deaf ears and let the strangers that whisper; sleep on the bed of lies that put crooks in their backs. The misaligned can't be aligned with authenticity. So just continue to remain true to yourself and keep pushing forward in the life you're living but never allow false information to ruin your vibe, your frequency, and your energy.

More importantly, however, is that you don't contribute to the whispers about someone else that

Noesis

you really don't know. Don't be what frustrates you; in fact, be better than that and either shut down the false narrative being created or step away from the conversation. If they who are talking ask you why you did that? Just tell them you don't participate in the tearing down of someone's character.

Understand; I'm not trying to be obtuse to how you might feel about the words that you might hear about your false self from someone speaking inaccurate information, but if you know those words hold no merit then you don't have to grin and bear it.

Furthermore, if a person doesn't have the desire to get to know the true you or re-acquaint themselves with you after a shift in the friendship, then you don't have to pretend to care, and you don't have to be the one to reach out to figure out what's going on. Move on in love until the alignment occurs.

Now, if the whispers are cutting deep because they hold some truths and not because a stranger said it then instead of getting angry with the people who've said it; get aligned with yourself and work on those issues. The worst kind of person to be is the kind of

132 | P a g e | | E m p o w e r i n g t h e G o d
W i t h i n Y o u

person who doesn't fix the very flaws they themselves see every day but are quick to call out others.

Look, I'm typically not a bible person, but somewhere in the bible, there's a passage that translates to don't be a hypocrite! First, remove the beam out of your own eye, and then you can see clearly to remove the speck out of your brother's eye. Regardless of the belief, that's some real information.

I write these words for anyone feeling isolated in their friendships and networks. I write these words for anyone trying to find their place in the relationships that they have yet to figure out. I write these words for anyone angry, sad and frustrated by the whispers of strangers.

I write these words for anyone wanting to pull back from their goal of doing things differently this year and onward. Don't you quit, don't you retreat, don't you put up your walls just because someone doesn't get you, doesn't appreciate you or doesn't fucks with you.

Noesis

Everyone isn't going to like you just like everyone doesn't like me. People have preconceived notions about who I am, and they've never had one face to face conversation with me. That's what people do and if I stopped being authentic just because of those people then the people I really care about will suffer and so will yours. I leave you with this. Bill Cosby will never be looked at the same again due to the rape cases, but one thing I'll never forget about him were these words he said, *"I don't know the key to success but the key to failure is trying to please everybody."* So why care about the whispers of strangers? Let go and elevate.

Cognition 27

"We were God enough believing we weren't Good enough; so we struggled stopping the self-sabotaging stuff."

In this cognition, I'm going to connect with you about relationships, self-sabotaging said relationships and believing you aren't good enough for healthy relationships. Honestly, part of our human experience while here on earth is to establish relationships with other human beings.

We're designed to connect, fall in love with and befriend people that will help us in this life experience. In order to empower the God in you completely; it's vital for you to develop a community of people that you love unconditionally and love you.

But, for many reasons that I'll discuss here shortly, millions of people are struggling relationally.

J.M. Barrie's character Peter Pan said, *"The moment you doubt whether you can fly, you cease forever to be able to do it,"* and lately I've been trying to understand how people develop the belief (even if unconsciously) that they aren't good enough to have healthy relationship. I've been pondering why perfectly "good enough" people doubt whether they can fly high in healthy relationships.

Truth be told, I take no pleasure in this endeavor because at one point in my life I too was a person who self-sabotaged their relationships, I too didn't believe I was worthy of a healthy relationship.

Still; lately I've been noticing a troubling trend among people but especially among modern-day daters and I'm wondering if their belief in their inability to fly has damaged them in the dating world forever. Obviously, the metaphor is not about flying at all, but instead, it's about the doubt that prevents you from even trying. It's about the fear of falling before you even launch, before you even understand and before you even get the opportunity to truly liftoff.

So naturally I've been trying to examine the unfortunate truth about people who self-sabotage relationships due to the fact that they don't believe they're good enough and of course the best way for me to do this is to examine my own life and then compare that to other people I know to determine some form of understanding about "not being good enough". It's a daunting task, and it's one that can't be answered in one cognition, but I do want to tackle one section of the many moving parts of the "not good enough personality flaw."

Question; what responsibility or role do we as daters play in trying to convince the person we're dating that they're good enough for us? That's the question that I'm going to try to find an answer to in this cognition because quite frankly I think there are many people self-sabotaging their relationships because ultimately, they don't believe they're good enough. So; is it up to us, the dater, partner and lover of the one who sabotages to help them through their issues? And if so, how much?

I remember at the end of my last relationship, my then-girlfriend said to me that she "realized that she'll never be good enough for me." I found this to be completely ridiculous, not because I didn't believe her words but because I never once said anything in a negative way towards her to make her feel that way about our relationship.

 In fact, I went out of my way to accept her as she was. I went out of my way to speak life into her and her living situation. I never once told her she wasn't good enough for me and never did any actions (as far as I'm aware) to make her feel like she wasn't.

Were there things that I saw that she could improve on? Absolutely, and I suggested things that could be done. Were there things that she saw that I could improve on? Absolutely, and I tried to change once she brought it to my attention but like many things i life; changing into something new takes dedication, fortitude, and a true desire to want to do better but more importantly it takes the belief that you can do better.

Noesis

Identifying things in your partner that can benefit them is natural. That's part of what being in a healthy relationship entails. Your partner should identify areas in your life that one, can be improved and two, that they can help you with. If your partner isn't identifying things that can be improved in your life, then they don't really care about your overall well-being. If you aren't identifying and suggesting things in the life of the person you're dating, then you don't really care about them or at the very least as much as you should. Why be together if it's all about staying the same?

Constant criticism is not the goal nor is that healthy, but partners can't get defensive when your partner tries to show you a better way to live. If you do, one can't help but wonder if you care about your very own happiness and believe me when I say that not caring about your happiness will frustrate your partner even more than you not receiving their advice.

Furthermore, there will always be a few things that your partner likes that you'll change towards because you want to please them. For example, maybe you like your man to have a little hair on his chest, or maybe you like your lady to wear a little bit of makeup and you suggest a slight change.

There's nothing wrong with that, and there's nothing wrong with you adapting and adopting small changes for the person you love. All of that is to be expected in relationships. If my lady tells me she likes a certain cologne over another cologne that I normally wear, then I'm going to wear the cologne she likes more often and not get defensive.

Still, with that said I often wonder if I didn't do enough to help my ex feel like she was good enough. I often wonder if I could have said more, shown more, and done more to make her feel come confident in the relationship. Was there anything I could have done to make her feel good enough? Do we have any responsibility to do so and would it make a difference?

As a person who lived much of his adult life as such person who thought he wasn't good enough, I can speak frankly to this experience, and I can speak absolute truth to sabotaging my previous relationship in my twenties, and I can say without a shadow of doubt that in my personal experience, there was nothing that those women could have done to make me feel completely at ease about my worthiness.

Those women could have told me how much they liked me, loved me and adored me every five minutes and it still wouldn't have given me the lift I needed. I still wouldn't have believed I could fly and I would have found a reason as to why it can't be. Like many people, I ran away from perfectly healthy relationships or found illogical excuses and convinced myself that they were valid reasons as to why they and I couldn't be.

Maybe you've been doing this as well, and maybe you've been blaming your ex-lovers as to why none of your relationships have worked but if there's one thing I know for sure it's that we always have to account for the common denominator, which is always ourselves.

You have to always account for yourself, your thoughts, your actions, and your old bad habits. You have to be aware when the thing that constantly sabotages your relationships tries to reestablish its dominance over you.

The main responsibility that a dater, partner or lover has in the development of someone is to speak life into them. They don't have to take on your burden, your flaws, your worries or your insecurities unless they want to and if they do; it's up to you to make quick changes so that it doesn't bring them down.

It's not up to the dater to convince you that you're good enough. It's up to you to know it to be true because if you're relying on other people to justify your good enough then you're giving up the control that only you should have. You're ultimately placing your worthiness in what other people think and view as good enough.

Why does this happen? The better question is *why a you allow it to happen*? Why do you believe that yo don't deserve someone who loves you? Why do you continue to allow those who don't live your life to control your life? Why do you continue to conspicuously go ghost the moment someone shows you your worthiness?

Noesis

If you're dating someone who does these things, it can be utterly frustrating right? It's maddening when you go out of your way to show your appreciation thinking you're making progress together and a month later you're back at square one or even worse. Why does this happen?

There are many reasons why people do this, and I believe that women have it harder for various reasons but comparing yourself to others and what they have is one of the biggest reasons as to why people don't feel good enough. Here are a few tips I call the Divine 9 that will help you understand that you're God enough.

The Divine Nine

1. Stop comparing yourself to other people.
2. Evaluate your past relationships and identify common problem areas that came up. Tackle them with ferocity.
3. Pay attention to your insecurities and stop them from gaining momentum when they show up in your new relationships again and then do the

opposite of what your insecurities make you feel like doing.

4. Try to remove your ego from the equation. Ask yourself if you have a valid reason to be bothered or is it just your ego trying to convince you that it isn't an ego bruise.

5. Get help! Find someone to talk with about the problems that you're dealing with mentally and listen to the feedback.

6. Work on your self-love.

7. Find closure on the issues from your childhood that are causing issues in your adulthood.

8. Find closure from your past relationships. Many people are continuing to allow people who are long gone to remain in present moments.

9. Bask in the compliments, acceptance, and love that your partner gives you. Live in those moments but more importantly TRUST in them.

May these words strike a chord inside anyone whose eyes have been glued to these pages. Understand from this moment on that you're more than good enough, *you're God enough because God is you, in*

you and created you. So unless you believe that God creates inferior versions of God-self, then you're going to have to come to grips with the fact that you're good enough for anyone and deserve the healthiest and happiest relationships that life can bring.

Cognition 28

"Built a temple that I owned and learned that I had to fix everything that was broken within it."

I want to end book 1 on a subject that millions of people are struggling with and it's a subject near and dear to my heart, spirit, and mind. I want to end book 1 with advice that I hope you apply to each aspect of your life but especially with each cognition in this book.

I'm going to get a little personal because I wouldn't be Jay Noetic if I didn't give you a little part of my life in my books. So, understand; I'm writing these words to prepare you for your next progression, and you aren't going to like it, but it's truly the best advice in this book.

Noesis

Throughout Noesis I've written from a perspective of a life coach, spiritual coach and motivational speaker with very little personal stories included. If you read my first book *The Unbelievable Truth: A Guide to Finding Peace,* you understand that in that book it was all my story and how I found peace. Noesis has not been that way by design. I've grown, I've evolved, I've gained better clarity and it was important not only in my development but in your development for me to write from a different perspective. This wisdom in this final cognition of book 1 can change your life when you apply it to EVERYTHING in your life. Are you ready?

In my three-year hiatus between my very first book and the one you're holding in your hands, I really had to evaluate my life and do some deep soul searching to try to find the reasons my life wasn't where I envisioned my life to be.

It was most certainly better than it had ever been but there were a lot of things that I still needed to do better with and so; I asked myself what the common issue in each aspect of my life was. I asked myself what choices led to my current situation and who was to blame for said situations.

It was there at the end of that evaluation that I realized that we ourselves are the reason we do or don't have the very things we say need the most. So, read these next words carefully; in fact; etch them into your mind.

The best philosophy that I ever learned and then adopted for my life was taking ownership of it. It single-handedly changed my entire life, and that's no exaggeration. The moment I started realizing how much power and control I had for MY life; I began t better my life.

It's easy to blame other people for why you're where you are in life, and people are quick to ask other people "why did you do this to me?" but the better question you should ask is "why did you do this to yourself?

No literally, when you find yourself in a situation th you dislike; reflect within by asking "why did you d this to yourself? The day I decided to own my shit f my failed relationships, poor credit, drama, utilities being disconnected or repossessed vehicles in the past and everything else that I wish I was no longer part of, I started coming out those situations.

It wasn't a coincidence that the changes happened the moment I took ownership of my ENTIRE life. It wasn't God bringing me out of the situations, and it wasn't the devil putting me into those situations. It was me, it was me, and it was me.

I took ownership for the good I had in my life as well as the bad things I had in my life. I stopped giving my power away, and I got to work on me, my unhealthy decisions and my laziness. I advise you reader to adopt this philosophy so that you can improve your situations.

The second most important philosophy that I earned and adopted was "controlling what I can control" and letting the rest go. Some of you call this "letting go and letting God" and I mean this with no disrespect but living by that motto takes away the God in you. It takes away everything that you control and truly it takes away the ONLY thing that you control. It sounds good in theory but, it can't hold its weight because it suggests that you let go and let God deal with it.

Why would you want to let go of something that affects your life massively and then just hope you can pray the situation away? I don't know what the definition of irresponsible is off the top of my head, but I'm pretty damn sure if we looked it up it would say something like "hoping we can pray shit away."

That takes away the power and control that you have over your life, and at the end of the day, you truly are in control of your life. You can let go and let God, but those issues will still exist, and the only way pass those issues is by you taking actions to do so.

You can't just let go and then not do something to bring you out of those situations. Faith without work is dead before it gets started. Life doesn't work that way, my friend. Understand that when I say let the rest go and give up control; I mean stop stressing over it and let it be until you're in a better place to own it and fix it. Own it from the jump and place it on the backburner until you're ready to take yourself out of that situation.

I can't prove that THE God is most powerful, but I can prove that you are. I can't prove that THE God fixes all things in your life, but I can prove that you do. I know it sucks being the common denominator but the good news about you always being part of the problem is that you're also always part of the solutions. And that my friend is powerful regardless of who or what you believe in. Take ownership and give up control of the uncontrollable.

Your entire life depends on it.

Noesis

"Sometimes you have to see beyond what you constantly see in order to fully understand what else is out there that may lead you to brave new worlds. New Discoveries aren't often made in your backyard nor on your front step; they are made when you go beyond what your eyes can see."

This book is dedicated to the people who read every page and to all of you who support me, believe in me and push me to be the best version of me.

Noesis

FOLLOW ME ON SOCIAL MEDIA

Instagram: Jay_Noetic

Blog: Anoeticlife.com

Twitter: Jnoetic

FaceBook:

Youtube:

Follow My Podcast: All Tea No Shade Podcast

Instagram: Allteanoshadepodcast

Streaming On: Spotify, Itunes, Soundcloud, IHeartradio & Stitcher

Art Work (Book Cover)

Isaiah Moffett is an talented young artist. I put a social media blast out on facebook asking my facebook friends if they knew anyone that talent that I could allow to shine along with me.

Many responded and the art on the front of this book immediately stood out to me and caught me eye. I knew the second I saw it that this would be the piece I would use for my book cover.

Isaiah Moffett is 19 years old, raised in Albuquerque, New Mexico and has been doing art since he was ab to use his hands. For the most part of his journey in art, he's been under looked because he thought he wasn't good enough.

But with practice everyday and living through the struggles of his life, he was able to find his inner strengths with painting and also master his expression with it. Now he's in the mix of making sure his art takes him to the highest levels he can reach.

Isaiah's art can be purchased so please follow him on Snapchat @hiipiiie and to purchase his art please email him at goldenhippie47@gmail.com.

~

Contact information for Bridgette Simmonds, PCC, CPC, ELI0MP Certified Life and Leadership Coach of InspHigher, LCC

www.bridgettethegocoach.com

37013604R00095

Made in the USA
Lexington, KY
20 April 2019